Contents

Why grow stuff?

Growing fantastic plants and flowers is a lot of fun. It doesn't have to be hard work, expensive or tricky to do – and you don't need a big garden. Try some of the ideas in this book and soon you'll be growing all kinds of cool stuff!

Cool Idea
Put dead plants in a **composter** or garden recycling bin. This means that even if your growing plans go wrong, the plants won't be wasted.

Stephanie Turnbull

W
FRANKLIN WATTS

An Appleseed Editions book

Paperback edition 2018
First published in 2015 by Franklin Watts

Created by Appleseed Editions Ltd,
Well House, Friars Hill, Guestling,
East Sussex TN35 4ET

Designed and illustrated by Guy Callaby
Edited by Mary-Jane Wilkins

ISBN 978-1-4451-4174-9
Dewey Classification: 635

A CIP catalogue for this book is available from the British Library.

Photo acknowledgements
t = top; c = centre; b = bottom; r = right; l = left
page 1 WilleeCole/Shutterstock; 2 Fotokostic/Shutterstock; 4 Goodluz/
Shutterstock; 5t shamek, bl Diana Taliun, br yuris/all Shutterstock; 6 iStock/
Thinkstock; 7tl and tr iStockphoto, bl Brand X Pictures, br Zoonar/ all Thinkstock;
8t Sandra van der Steen/Shutterstock, b Mim Waller; 9t Mim Waller,
b Kenishirotie/Shutterstock; 10 tl Reika, Jiri Hera, tr iStockphoto/Thinkstock,
l Nagy-Bagoly Arpad, b Bennyartist/both Shutterstock; 11 iStockphoto/
Thinkstock; 12t Tomas Loutocky, l and c marilyn barbone/all Shutterstock,
r iStockphoto, bl Zoonar, bc and br iStockphoto/all Thinkstock; 13 B. and E.
Dudzinscy/Shutterstock; 14t Zoonar/Thinkstock, bl Tom Biegalski, bc left to right
haraldmuc, Vilor, Peter Zijlstra, Lusoimages/all Shutterstock, bees iStockphoto/
Thinkstock; 15t Hemera, r, bl and br iStockphoto/all Thinkstock; 16t Valeria73, by
Paul/both Shutterstock; 17c Mim Waller, b africanstuff/Shutterstock; 18t Hellen
Sergeyeva, tr Shane White, l Mamuka Gotsiridze/all Shutterstock; 19 Tamara
Kulikova/Shutterstock; 20l DL Pohl, r Samo Trebizan/both Shutterstock;
21t Reika, b Kisialiou Yury/both Shutterstock; 22t udra11, bl Cora Mueller,
br David Fowler/all Shutterstock; 23t Robyn Mackenzie, b Yu Lan/both
Shutterstock; 24t iStockphoto/Thinkstock, b rodho/Shutterstock; 25t Edward
Westmacott/Shutterstock, b Mim Waller; 26t c.byatt-norman, l M. Cornelius,
c Africa Studio, r Tamara Kulikova/all Shutterstock; 27 kotkot32/Shutterstock;
28 Mim Waller; 29l Jason Swalwell/Shutterstock, r Mim Waller; 30t Madlen,
b Becky Stares/both Shutterstock; 31 Comstock Images/Thinkstock
lightbulb in Cool Ideas boxes Designs Stock/Shutterstock
Cover Maria Pavlova/Thinkstock

Printed in China

MIX
Paper from
responsible sources
FSC® C104740
www.fsc.org

Franklin Watts
An imprint of Hachette Children's Group
Part of The Watts Publishing Group
Carmelite House
50 Victoria Embankment
London EC4Y 0DZ

An Hachette UK Company
www.hachette.co.uk

www.franklinwatts.co.uk

Indoor blooms

How about keeping a few house plants to brighten up your bedroom? Many indoor plants are easy to look after and have amazing flowers. Good ones to try include kalanchoe, tropical **bromeliads** and Christmas or Easter flowering cacti.

Did You Know?

*Indoor plants remove **carbon dioxide** from the air and reduce air pollution – so they're good for you, too!*

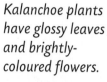

Kalanchoe plants have glossy leaves and brightly-coloured flowers.

Outdoor plants

You can grow all kinds of outdoor plants in window boxes or pots. If you have a garden, ask for a small area for your own plant experiments. Try growing a range of seeds and small plants and see what works best.

Delphiniums　　　*Courgettes*

Get growing!

Most seeds and plants come with instructions on how to care for them, so it makes sense to read and follow any advice. Here are a few essential facts and safety tips.

Plant basics

Plants need sunlight to grow (some more than others), so look for light, bright spots. They also need regular watering so the soil feels damp to the touch – not bone dry or soggy!

Check your plants every few days and pull out any weeds before they take over.

Use a small watering can with a thin spout for indoor plants. A big watering can with a spray spout is good for covering large outdoor pots or flower beds.

Use a bottle spray for seeds and very small plants, so you don't drown or flatten them.

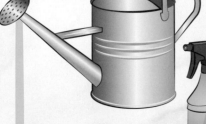

Cool Idea

Find a large box to store all your gardening gear and make sure you take it inside when you're not using it. Rusty tools are no good!

Did You Know?

Some plants, such as laburnum, yew and oleander, are poisonous. Never eat anything you grow unless you know it's edible and you've washed it well.

Laburnum

Cool compost

You can put plants straight into soil from the garden, but it makes a big difference to add **compost**, especially if you're planting in a pot. Compost contains a mix of **nutrients** that help plants grow big and strong.

Stay safe

When you're gardening, be careful with sharp tools and prickly plants, don't try to lift heavy things and ask an adult for help if you need it. Tidy up your stuff and ALWAYS wash your hands afterwards.

Wear gardening gloves, especially when planting bulbs, as they can irritate your skin.

No-soil planting

You may have grown cress seeds on damp cotton wool, but did you know that other plants grow without soil, too? Watching things grow in water is great because you can see roots clearly – and it doesn't involve any digging.

Floating foliage

Try this easy growing activity to get you started.

1. With a sharp knife, carefully chop the tops off a few turnips. You could also try carrots or parsnips.

2. Pour some water in a saucer, tray or shallow bowl and stand the turnip tops in the water, cut ends down.

3. Leave the saucer in a bright, warm place and watch leaves shoot out in just a few days. Soon you'll have floating islands of greenery!

Cool Idea

*Try using **organic** vegetables, as they may sprout faster.*

Hyacinth bulbs are often grown and displayed in clear vases of water.

Top up the water every few days as the turnip tops will soak it up.

Potato plant

For another great experiment try putting a sweet potato in water and tracking its growth. It takes a few weeks to start, but will then become a big, bushy plant!

1. *Fill a jar or glass with water and place a sweet potato in it, pointed end down. Push cocktail sticks into the potato to hold it over the water. About 5 cm should be in the water.*

2. *After a few weeks a thin, white root will appear, with smaller side roots growing off it. Soon more roots will snake out into the water.*

3. *Eventually shoots will sprout at the top of the potato.*

Did You Know?

*The science of growing plants in water containing **minerals** is called **hydroponics**. NASA scientists are experimenting with it as a way of growing fresh fruit and vegetables on future space missions.*

Put your sweet potato on a sunny windowsill and top up the water regularly. Leaves grow towards the sun, so turn the glass every week to stop them leaning too far.

Easy seeds

Annuals are plants that grow from seed, make flowers and die the same year – so a lot happens in a short time! Read seed packets and choose ones that are easy to grow.

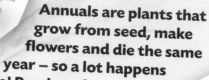

Sweet peas

Sunflower seeds

Poppy seeds

In or out?

Early in the year you can sow seeds in trays to **germinate** on a windowsill, then plant them outside when it's warmer. In late spring or early summer, seeds can go straight into soil or pots outside. All they need is about 12 mild, frost-free weeks to grow and flower.

Seedlings are tiny and very delicate at first.

Perfect planting

Here's how to get started. Label pots and keep the packet to remind you what you've planted.

1. *Set a clean seed tray or small pot on newspaper. Put in an equal amount of soil and compost, rubbing it between your hands to break up lumps and add air. This helps water drain through the mixture and allows roots to spread.*

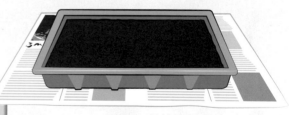

2. *Water the soil and scatter seeds evenly across it. Don't push them in – they need to be close to the surface. Sprinkle on more soil to cover them.*

Did You Know?

Annuals grow masses of flowers to make as many seeds (in flowers) as they can for next year. If you cut off dead flowers, the plant produces new ones – so keep snipping through the summer!

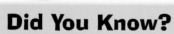

Make sure all the seeds are covered.

3. Water with a spray bottle and put the container on a bright, warm windowsill. Keep the soil damp with regular watering. Cover it with a clear plastic bag to keep moisture inside – but remove the bag once seeds sprout, or they may rot.

4. As the seedlings grow, pinch out a few smaller ones to give the bigger ones more space.

Some seed trays come with clear plastic covers.

5. When the shoots have a few leaves, carefully loosen the soil around them and take them out gently, trying not to tear the roots. Plant them in bigger pots (prepared as in step 1) or outside.

Cool Idea

Mix tiny seeds with sand before sowing. This stops them clumping too closely together.

Healthy herbs

Many herbs are easy to grow from seed on a windowsill or outside. They look good, smell fantastic and taste great.

Grow just one type of herb in each pot, or some will crowd out others.

Lavender

Lemon balm

Chives

Rosemary

What to try

Test the smell and taste of different cut herbs from the supermarket to decide which you like best. Buy seeds and sow them as on page 10, or buy small plants instead. Coriander, basil, chives, thyme and mint all grow well.

Anise hyssop

Coriander

Did You Know?

Romans believed that eating mint kept you calm and made you more intelligent. Try it yourself and see if they were right!

Great growing

Once your herbs are growing well, pick leaves from the top. This makes the plant produce more leaves and grow bushier. Pinch out any flowers – they take the plant's energy away from producing leaves!

Herby pasta

Herbs add flavour to curries and sauces. One easy recipe is to cook a pan of pasta, drain off the water, then add a little olive oil or butter and a few torn-up herb leaves such as basil or coriander. Heat it for a minute then eat it while it's hot. Delicious!

Sweet stuff

Herbs can flavour sweet things, too. One of the best is mint. Try this easy mint syrup that makes vanilla ice cream taste fantastic!

Try adding a jar of pesto sauce to your pasta and fresh basil.

1. *Pour 250 ml water into a pan and add 100g sugar. Heat gently to dissolve the sugar.*

2. *Pick a big handful of mint leaves. Wash and tear them up, then add to the pan.*

3. *Let the mixture boil and simmer for about ten minutes. Leave to cool, then pour a little over ice cream.*

Cool Idea

If you don't want big pieces of mint in the syrup, strain it through a sieve when cool.

Cool blooms

A mass of colourful flowers can brighten up your day! Here are some of the best flowering plants to look for in garden centres or supermarkets and then display in pots or a small flower bed.

Annuals such as petunias will grow and flower all summer as long as you water them regularly.

Cool Idea

Pick a few of your flowers and press them between heavy books for a few weeks to dry, then display them in a frame.

Amazing annuals

You can't beat annuals (see page 10) for lots of summer flowers. Tiny yellow and purple violas grow and spread all summer, then sow their own seeds for next year. Marigolds, cosmos and petunias look good for months.

Cosmos

Viola

Chocolate cosmos (which really does smell of chocolate!)

Marigold

Great geraniums

Geraniums are cheap, easy to grow and have dazzling red, pink, peach or white flowers. The secret to making them flower is to look for tiny new leaves...

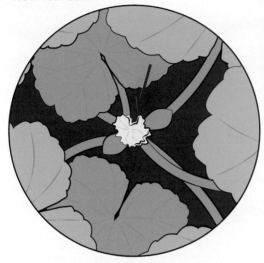

... and carefully nip them off with your fingernails.

This makes the plant produce flowers instead!

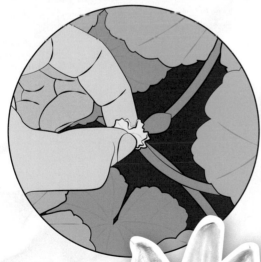

Passion flower

Did You Know?

Rafflesia arnoldii flowers are about a metre wide, making them the biggest flowers on Earth. But you wouldn't want to grow them... they stink of rotting flesh to attract flies.

Crazy shapes

How about growing more unusual flowers? Bleeding hearts are so called because they look like hearts with a delicate drop of 'blood'. Fuchsias are a hanging teardrop shape and come in all colours and sizes. Passion flowers have so many complicated parts that they don't look real!

Fuchsia

Bleeding heart

Rock gardens

Alpines are small, spreading plants that grow wild on steep mountain sides. Here's how you can create your own mini mountain environment for alpines in your back garden.

Cold and dry

Alpines may look delicate, but they can survive extremely low temperatures. The one thing they hate is being wet. This means it's important to give them soil that allows water to drain through easily.

Did You Know?

Japanese rock gardens are elegant arrangements of rocks, gravel, plants and water features designed to make you calm and relaxed.

Beautiful alpine flowers cover the slopes of mountains as soon as the snow melts in spring.

Let's rock!

Here's how to construct a rock garden that will give alpines a perfect home.

1. *Find a large pot and line it with stones or broken pieces of pot (to help drainage).*

2. *Fill it with equal amounts of soil and **grit** mixed together.*

3. *Find a few big stones and arrange them on the top.*

4. *Buy three alpines to plant around the stones. Don't plant too many as they will spread as they grow. **Succulents** look great and grow well.*

5. *Fill gaps with pebbles. Water the pot to help the plants start growing.*

Cool Idea

Use decorative or shiny rocks and pebbles to make your rock garden look really special.

Clever cuttings

Many gardeners grow new plants by taking cuttings from older, bigger ones. It saves money and isn't too difficult. Why not have a try?

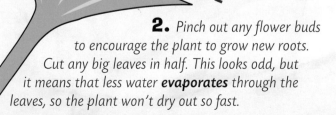

What to use

Two of the best plants to use for cuttings are geraniums (see page 15) and a type of trailing house plant called tradescantia. This has dark purple leaves and grows so fast it soon covers its pot completely!

Start snipping

This type of cutting is best taken in spring or early summer when plants are growing fast. Here's what to do.

Cool Idea

Take several cuttings at once to give you more chance of success. Space them around one wide pot, then move them to separate pots when they're bigger.

1. *Find a small, healthy new shoot and cut it off just below a leaf. Carefully nip off the lowest leaves (this section will go under the soil).*

2. *Pinch out any flower buds to encourage the plant to grow new roots. Cut any big leaves in half. This looks odd, but it means that less water **evaporates** through the leaves, so the plant won't dry out so fast.*

3. Fill a pot with soil and compost (see page 10) and water it. Make a hole near the side with a pencil, then carefully put in your cutting and firm the soil around it so it doesn't fall over.

4. Water the pot carefully and put it on a warm windowsill. Soon, new roots should grow, followed by leaves.

Did You Know?

Just one leaf from an African violet can grow into a whole new plant if you stick it into soil!

Brilliant bulbs

Bulbs are amazing – they contain all the nutrients they need to transform into magnificent flowers such as daffodils, tulips and alliums. Some, such as amaryllis, will grow on a sunny windowsill, but most do best outdoors.

This amaryllis bulb has just started to sprout thick, broad leaves.

Cool Idea

Tulips and daffodils look great when there are lots of them, so the more you plant the better. For a natural look, scatter a big handful on the ground and plant them where they fall.

Daffodils

Top bulb tips

Most bulbs need planting in autumn and start to grow in spring when the weather is warmer. Here are a few secrets for growing great bulbs.

1. *Get them the right way up!* The pointy end is where the stem will grow, so it should face upwards. If you can't tell which end is which, plant bulbs on their side. The stem will find its way upwards.

2. Don't let pots get soggy. Add grit to your soil and compost to help drainage – you don't want your bulbs to rot!

3. Dig deep. Bulbs need to be buried at least three times their own height. Make sure your hole is deep enough before you put in the bulb and cover it with soil.

4. Watch out for wildlife. Mice and squirrels love to nibble bulbs, so you may need to cover pots or flower beds with chicken wire. Ask an adult to help with this.

Did You Know?

Some plants grow from corms, rhizomes, roots or tubers, which are fat, round plant stems that often look like bulbs. They are usually planted in the same way.

Ginger roots

5. Snip off dead flowers – but not the leaves. When bulbs finish flowering, their leaves help make food to store for next year's flowers. Dead leaves will eventually shrivel and disappear.

Tulips

Fantastic food

There are loads of different fruits and vegetables to grow. Choose things you like to eat and check whether they are suited to the climate where you live.

Super salads

If you only have a windowsill, try growing salad leaves. Plant them in the same way as herbs and cut leaves as soon as they look ready. Add them to sandwiches or mix them with salad dressing.

Experiment with different types and colours of salad leaves.

Juicy fruit

Strawberries taste great and aren't hard to grow. They need a sunny, sheltered spot, but not much space, so you can grow them in a pot, window box or in the ground. You may need some netting to protect fruit from hungry birds!

Only pick strawberries that are red all over.

Sacks of spuds

Potatoes are also fun to grow. Buy **seed potatoes** and check what time of year to plant and harvest them.

1. First, stand your potatoes in an egg box in a warm, sunny place for a few days until small, knobbly sprouts appear. This is called **chitting**.

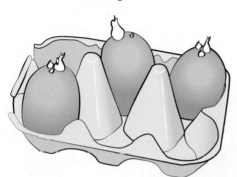

2. Find a large, empty compost bag or rubble sack. Roll down the sides to about a third of its height, then fill it with compost. Ask an adult to poke a few holes in the bottom of the bag so water can drain out.

3. Place five potatoes with knobbly bits upwards and cover them with about 10 cm of compost.

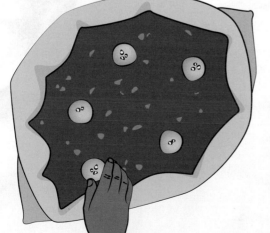

Cool Idea

Make a meal out of potatoes by scrubbing them and pricking holes with a fork. Bake them at 200°C (180°C fan oven, 400°F, gas mark 6) for about an hour, then add toppings such as cream cheese, tuna, ham or grated cheese. Serve with home-grown salad or herbs.

4. After a few weeks, potato plants will sprout. Cover them with more compost. Keep doing this as the plants grow, gradually unrolling the sides of the bag to make it taller.

Don't forget to water the bag regularly.

5. When the soil is nearly at the top of the bag, let the plants grow bushy. Potatoes will form under the soil. When the plants begin to flower, carefully dig up the potatoes with a fork or trowel.

Did You Know?

Growing potatoes need to be kept covered with soil because light turns them green – and green potatoes are poisonous!

Mini gardens

Why not create your own fantastic miniature garden? You'll need a selection of small plants, pebbles, small toys or doll's house furniture – and plenty of imagination.

1. First, find a wide pot or window box. Make sure it has holes in the bottom for water to drain out. Fill the pot with a mixture of soil and compost.

2. Now collect a few small plants. Look for short, tiny-leaved varieties such as lobelia, alyssum or thyme. These are often sold in packs of four or six **plug plants**, which are just the size you need.

Plug plants of alyssum

3. Plan a design. You could have a winding path through the middle and a patio area at one side. Plant your flowers, making sure they aren't too close together as they'll soon spread.

Did You Know?

Bonsai is the Japanese art of growing miniature trees in pots. The trees need to be carefully pruned, trimmed and watered.

4. Now add small, flat stones to make the patio and path, with pebbles or gravel to fill in the gaps.

Cool Idea

If your mini garden plants die, add plastic Halloween toys to make a spooky dead garden!

5. Add features such as toy chairs or wheelbarrows. Try using farm models such as fences or chickens, a cocktail umbrella for a sun shade, or bottle lids for mini pots. Moss makes a good lawn.

Cool containers

Plant pots don't have to be brown and boring!
As long as they have drainage holes, you can
grow plants in any container – even old
shoes or Wellington boots!

*Look for unusual
containers to
stand pots
inside.*

Get decorating

Liven up plain **terracotta** or plastic pots by painting them with bright **acrylic paints** or sticking on shells or ribbon with craft glue. Decorate yoghurt pots in the same way, then plant small flowers in each and give them away as gifts.

NAOMI

Pot people

Here's a really easy way of creating a potty person to cheer up your garden!

1. *Plant a bushy plant in a plain terracotta pot. This will be your pot person's head. Find a bigger pot for the body, turn it upside down and put the smaller pot on top.*

Cool Idea

Give pots extra colour by making bright plant markers from lolly sticks. Write the name of the plant on each stick then decorate it with stickers or shiny gift ribbons.

Did You Know?

Terracotta pots soak up water easily, which means that they may crack in winter as water freezes and expands. Bring yours inside in winter if you live in a cold place.

2. *Draw a face using marker pens, or stick on googly eyes with craft glue. Add features such as buttons, old scarves and jewellery. Make some more flowerpot friends to keep your pot person company.*

Standing high up like this will give your pot excellent drainage – and it will be out of reach of most slugs, too.

Arty ideas

Use your growing skills to get creative in the garden and design something amazing!

Grass letters

Make your mark by displaying your initials in grass.

1. Find a seed tray and fill it with a mixture of soil and compost. Crumble it through your fingers (see page 10) to get rid of big lumps. Water the soil so it's moist.

2. With your finger or a stick, draw your initial in the soil. Make the lines thick. If you have space, do your whole name or make a pattern, too.

3. Carefully sprinkle plenty of grass seeds in the grooves. Use a funnel to avoid scattering seeds everywhere.

4. Cover the seeds with a thin layer of crumbled soil. Water gently so seeds aren't washed away.

5. Watch your design appear over the next few weeks. Don't let the soil dry out!

When the grass is long, trim it with scissors to keep it neat.

Use a bottle spray to water the seeds.

 Cool Idea

Secretly make a grass pattern or word for a friend and give them the tray with instructions to water it regularly. As the grass grows, your surprise will be revealed!

Ivy sculpting

Ivy is a fast-growing, creeping plant that will climb up anything it can cling to or twine around. It's perfect for making sculptures.

1. Open out and reshape a wire coat hanger to make a circle. Straighten the curved end of the hanger.

2. Push the end of the hanger firmly into the middle of a pot of ivy. Gently wind the ends of the ivy around the wire hoop.

As the ivy grows, wind it around the hoop. Tuck in any stray ends.

Cool Idea

Hang a bauble or small wind chime from the hoop for a finishing touch.

Did You Know?

The art of clipping trees or bushes to make neat shapes is called topiary. Experts create amazing animals, faces, people and even complicated shapes such as bicycles!

Glossary

acrylic paints
Fast-drying paints that can be mixed with water or used straight from the tube. Be careful as they won't wash off clothes when dry!

bromeliad
A type of tropical plant that often grows flowers on tall stalks with wide, colourful leaves called bracts.

carbon dioxide
A gas in the air around us. We breathe out carbon dioxide, and plants absorb it as part of their food-making process.

chitting
Letting seed potatoes germinate in a warm place before they are planted.

compost
Rotted plants and other natural materials. Good compost is crumbly and dark, with an earthy smell.

composter
A metal, wooden or plastic bin in which plants and other garden waste rot and turn into compost.

evaporate
To change from a liquid or solid to a gas.

germinate
To begin to grow.

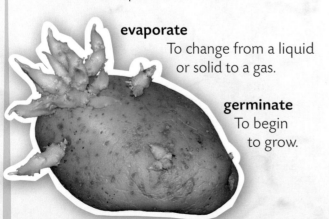

grit
Tiny bits of sand or stone.

minerals
Natural substances from the ground.

nutrients
Good, healthy substances found in compost that help plants grow well. Minerals are a type of nutrient.

organic
Food which is grown using only natural products, without any artificial pest sprays or chemical fertilizers.

plug plant
A small plant which already has a few roots and leaves. Plug plants are useful to buy when you don't want to grow plants from seeds.

seed potato
A specially grown, disease-free potato tuber designed to produce healthy potatoes when planted. An ordinary potato from the supermarket won't produce such a good crop.

succulent
A plant with thick, fleshy leaves or stems that store water. They grow well in dry places such as rock gardens.

terracotta
Hard, orange-brown clay, often made into plant pots.

Websites

www.rhs.org.uk/education-learning/gardening-children-schools/family-activities/grow-it
Explore the Grow it! section of the RHS children and schools website.

www.which.co.uk/reviews/grow-your-own/article/guides
Learn how to grow vegetables that are easy to look after and don't take up much space.

www.nationaltrust.org.uk/lists/50-things-activities-in-your-back-garden
Find all sorts of ways to have fun in your own back garden with the National Trust's list of activities for children.

www.thecraftycrow.net/garden
Check out brilliantly arty ideas for making plant markers and much more.

Index